Acting Edition

Thespian Playworks 2020

Consequential Strangers
by Kea Kamiya

Love is Blind
by Aiko Lozar

Sunday Afternoon Gin
by Josie Palmarini

The Firefly Hour
by Taylor Lockhart

Consequential Strangers Copyright © 2021 by Kea Kamiya
Love is Blind Copyright © 2021 by Aiko Lozar
Sunday Afternoon Gin Copyright © 2021 by Josie Palmarini
The Firefly Hour Copyright © 2021 by Taylor Lockhart
All Rights Reserved

THESPIAN PLAYWORKS 2020 is fully protected under the copyright laws of the United States of America, the British Commonwealth, including Canada, and all member countries of the Berne Convention for the Protection of Literary and Artistic Works, the Universal Copyright Convention, and/or the World Trade Organization conforming to the Agreement on Trade Related Aspects of Intellectual Property Rights. All rights, including professional and amateur stage productions, recitation, lecturing, public reading, motion picture, radio broadcasting, television and the rights of translation into foreign languages are strictly reserved.

ISBN 978-0-573-70949-4

www.concordtheatricals.com
www.concordtheatricals.co.uk

FOR PRODUCTION ENQUIRIES

UNITED STATES AND CANADA
info@concordtheatricals.com
1-866-979-0447

UNITED KINGDOM AND EUROPE
licensing@concordtheatricals.co.uk
020-7054-7200

Each title is subject to availability from Concord Theatricals, depending upon country of performance. Please be aware that *THESPIAN PLAYWORKS 2020* may not be licensed by Concord Theatricals in your territory. Professional and amateur producers should contact the nearest Concord Theatricals office or licensing partner to verify availability.

CAUTION: Professional and amateur producers are hereby warned that *THESPIAN PLAYWORKS 2020* is subject to a licensing fee. Publication of this play(s) does not imply availability for performance. Both amateurs and professionals considering a production are strongly advised to apply to Concord Theatricals before starting rehearsals, advertising, or booking a theater. A licensing fee must be paid whether the title(s) is presented for charity or gain and whether or not admission is charged. Professional/Stock licensing fees are quoted upon application to Concord Theatricals.

This work is published by Samuel French, an imprint of Concord Theatricals.

No one shall make any changes in this title(s) for the purpose of production. No part of this book may be reproduced, stored in a retrieval system, or transmitted in any form, by any means, now known or yet to be invented, including mechanical, electronic, photocopying, recording, videotaping, or otherwise, without the prior written permission of the publisher. No one shall upload this title(s), or part of this title(s), to any social media websites.

For all enquiries regarding motion picture, television, and other media rights, please contact Concord Theatricals.

MUSIC USE NOTE

Licensees are solely responsible for obtaining formal written permission from copyright owners to use copyrighted music in the performance of this play and are strongly cautioned to do so. If no such permission is obtained by the licensee, then the licensee must use only original music that the licensee owns and controls. Licensees are solely responsible and liable for all music clearances and shall indemnify the copyright owners of the play(s) and their licensing agent, Concord Theatricals, against any costs, expenses, losses and liabilities arising from the use of music by licensees. Please contact the appropriate music licensing authority in your territory for the rights to any incidental music.

IMPORTANT BILLING AND CREDIT REQUIREMENTS

If you have obtained performance rights to this title, please refer to your licensing agreement for important billing and credit requirements.

ABOUT THESPIAN PLAYWORKS

Thespian Playworks is a writing contest and script development program for high school students, sponsored by the Educational Theatre Association and run by the staff of *Dramatics* magazine. Each year, up to four finalists are invited to the International Thespian Festival, where the students work with a professional director, a dramaturg, and a volunteer cast of actors to put their short plays on their feet before a live audience.

Launched in 1994 as a tribute to longtime International Thespian Society executive Doug Finney, the program aims to nurture young playwrights, and over Playworks' history, many participants have gone on to college majors and careers in theatre, writing, and related fields. Whatever the eventual future of the writers or their scripts, Playworks is an exhilarating experience in a creative discipline seldom taught in schools or celebrated in the wider culture.

The call for entries goes out each fall, with submission deadlines in mid-winter. *Dramatics* receives scores of scripts from high school Thespians all over the U.S., Canada, and as far away as the United Arab Emirates. Each play is reviewed at least twice, as teams of readers (including *Dramatics* staff and other professional critics and theatre artists) narrow down the entries: first to a dozen semifinalists, then to the final four. Each semifinalist receives a personal letter with feedback on their script.

In 2021, Thespian Playworks will be rebranded as part of the International Thespian Excellence Awards. For more on the new program, please visit https://thespys.org.

CONTENTS

Consequential Strangers 1
Love is Blind 15
Sunday Afternoon Gin 93
The Firefly Hour 105

CONSEQUENTIAL STRANGERS

Kea Kamiya

CONSEQUENTIAL STRANGERS was produced virtually during the 2020 Virtual International Thespian Festival.

CHARACTERS

ROB – an outgoing man in his early thirties
JAMES – a burdened man in his early thirties

SETTING

America, takes place in a public men's bathroom

TIME

Present Day

(Men's bathroom.)

*(**ROB** is washing his hands at a sink. **JAMES** enters, holding his baby, Nessa, and wearing a backpack. **JAMES** looks around and sighs. He experiments with crouching and tries to balance Nessa on his knees. **ROB** tries not to stare. **JAMES** decides to change his tactic. He goes to set Nessa on the ground. **ROB** is cringing.)*

ROB. Try the sink! Trust me, you don't want to put your baby on that floor.

*(The two **MEN** stare at each other for a second.)*

JAMES. You're right. I just wasn't sure the sink would be much cleaner.

*(**ROB** shrugs. **JAMES** brings Nessa over to the sink counter and lays her down. Nessa's head almost falls into the sink.)*

Ah!

*(On instinct, **ROB** reaches out and helps to keep her from falling.)*

ROB. Sorry, uh, here, lemme...uh...

JAMES. Thanks.

ROB. No problem.

*(**JAMES** helps to hold Nessa. He looks down at his daughter, and then at the diaper in his hand. He sighs.)*

ROB. Uh, you good?

JAMES. Yeah.

> *(He stares, trying to figure out how to go about this.)*

Uh, have you ever changed a diaper before?

ROB. Not in a men's restroom.

> *(He notices the emblem on **JAMES'** polo.)*

Nice shirt. You work for Squeaky Clean?

JAMES. Well, uh, actually, I use–

ROB. That's where I work! We're probably here for the same dinner. If you tell me what your wife looks like, I can go tell her that you need help. I'm Rob, by the way.

> *(He's beaming with good intentions and **JAMES** looks like he wants to die.)*

JAMES. James and Nessa. Uh, thank you. But, uh, I don't – I'm not married.

ROB. Oh, I'm sorry. Your girlfriend?

JAMES. Don't have one of those either.

ROB. This is your baby, right?

> *(**JAMES** gives **ROB** a look.)*

JAMES. Thank you for trying to help me, but I don't really know you and I don't want you to feel like you have to. I'm sure I can figure out how to change her diaper myself.

> *(Just then, Nessa starts to slide off the sink. Both the **MEN** lunge forward to catch her.)*

ROB. C'mon man. If you work for Squeaky Clean you're already family! It can't be that hard, right?

JAMES. Right. Well, I guess you just...start.

(**JAMES** *sets the clean diaper in the corner of the sink. He starts to tug at the bottom of Nessa's pants. The two* **MEN** *stand in silence until* **ROB** *can't take it anymore.*)

ROB. So, uh, you're watching the baby for your ex?

JAMES. Not exactly.

(*He isn't excited to share more, but* **ROB** *looks at him expectantly.*)

I have full custody.

ROB. Oh. Good for you.

(**JAMES** *gets Nessa's pants off and holds them.* **ROB** *takes them out of his hand.*)

JAMES. It's just, my mom's been helping me since my wife left, and I'm still getting the hang of it.

ROB. I'm sorry about your wife, man.

JAMES. Yeah. Sorry. You didn't need to know that. I guess I'm practicing my "spill my deepest baggage to strangers" skills.

(**JAMES** *is struggling with the clasps on the onesie.*)

ROB. No, it's just...at least you don't have to pay child support, right?

JAMES. Well, there's always that. Damn! How many little metal claspy things do they have to put on these! Here can you help –

(*He gestures to the baby's head.*)

ROB. Yeah, sure.

(**JAMES** *finally gets the clasps undone.*)

JAMES. Got it!

(**JAMES** *stares for a second.*)

ROB. What?

JAMES. I just realized we are just now getting to the actual diaper.

ROB. How are you supposed to get it off?

JAMES. Maybe you can just shimmy it down?

(**JAMES** *tries this method, which does not work.*)

ROB. Shouldn't there be like a diaper button? Like jeans have a button and a zipper?

JAMES. Hmmm...found it! Flaps. There are little flaps!

(*They nod, proud of each other and their accomplishment.* **JAMES** *removes the diaper and they both recoil, coughing.*)

ROB. We should be wearing gloves.

JAMES. And a gas mask.

(*Beat.*)

I think I need the wipes. Can you uh –

(*He gestures to the baby.*)

– for a second?

ROB. What? Oh, sure.

(*He supports Nessa, and* **JAMES** *rummages in the bag.* **ROB** *really looks into Nessa's little face.*)

(*Mostly to himself.*) How could she just leave her kid like that?

(*Beat.*)

I knew this guy from high school, has kids with like three different women in three different states. He just pays child support and keeps living his life. How the hell do you do that?

JAMES. I don't know. I guess…some people just don't think it'll make them happy.

(He retrieves the wipes and stands back up.)

(He looks at his baby, the wipes, and the current position of the diaper.)

Now how do I…

ROB. I actually know this. I've seen someone do this. You grab her feet.

JAMES. You do what?

ROB. Yeah, no that's really what you do, you grab her feet and like lift her up, and then you can get the diaper and stuff.

JAMES. I feel like babies aren't supposed to bend like that.

*(**ROB** shrugs.)*

ROB. I don't know, man. I'm pretty sure you're supposed to do that.

*(**JAMES** tentatively utilizes this method – and it works!)*

JAMES. Thanks. I think I can figure it out from here. I mean, you can go, I feel bad for keeping you.

ROB. Oh no, it's really no problem. I want to stay and help.

JAMES. I'm serious, man. I mean, thank you for the help, but I feel really bad for keeping you –

ROB. Dude, why are you being so pushy? I'm trying to help you. Just let me help!

JAMES. Okay.

(Beat.)

Are you hiding?

(As he speaks, he wipes Nessa.)

ROB. What?

JAMES. I've never spoken to another dude in a public bathroom, let alone had one offer to help me change my daughter's diaper. Then I ask you to leave and you have a moment? There's some reason you don't want to be out there and you're hanging out in the bathroom to avoid it.

*(He has gotten the old diaper off and rolls it up and hands it to **ROB**. **JAMES** is proud of himself for having figured this out.)*

ROB. Hey! I just wanted to be a good person. Squeaky Clean is like my family. I wanted to help you! It's not your fault that they don't put changing tables in men's restrooms. I was trying to help you out, dude, and now you're accusing me? It's a free country. I'm just hanging out in a bathroom, helping a stranger change his daughter's diaper...on a sink. That's, that's normal. That's fine.

*(**ROB** throws the diaper away.)*

JAMES. Just seemed weird to me.

ROB. Yeah, well, you don't have to attack people. And the audacity, I mean we work at the same company for goodness sakes –

JAMES. I – I actually don't work for Squeaky Clean. I mean, I don't anymore.

ROB. What? Then what are you doing here?

JAMES. Reliving my glory days. Look, I was top sales manager for years and when I was working as a representative...well let's just say I once sold 50,000 gallons of dish soap in a week. You say Squeaky is like your family, but, man, you don't even know. And, you know, part of me wants to know what downstairs airhead they'll put in my old position.

(**JAMES** *chuckles, but* **ROB** *is stone-faced.*)

ROB. You think they'll promote an airhead, huh?

JAMES. Well I mean –

ROB. I'm getting promoted.

(*Beat.*)

JAMES. You're kidding.

ROB. Nope. You're right. I'm not just staying here to be helpful. Hell, I haven't even been much help. I'm getting promoted, to, I guess, your old job and I just can't face them. I'm the airhead.

JAMES. You just can't face success?

ROB. That's not it.

JAMES. If you don't want the job, don't take the promotion.

ROB. Trust me, I don't want to take it! I didn't know it was you.

JAMES. It doesn't matter. You should take it, if you want it. But if you don't want it...

ROB. I'm not trying to sound ungrateful. I just feel like I have to take the job. My wife's already started planning a new kitchen and she gets so upset about "missed opportunities"...she would be pissed.

JAMES. You're going to take a job you don't want because of pre-planned countertops?

ROB. No, but I might take a job I don't want to keep my wife happy. We just got married. She still looks at me like I could fix anything. And, it would be easy to fix this. Everybody has to make sacrifices, right? Bet you'd know about that.

JAMES. Uh. Yeah. But for the record, making sacrifices doesn't mean surrendering control over your whole life. You still get a say.

(He turns back to Nessa and puts the new diaper under her. He fiddles with it.)

ROB. I guess. I'm sorry about getting your old job.

JAMES. Don't be. You don't even know me. And I know it's pathetic, wearing my old company shirt, dragging my daughter here, but I came because I wanted to know who they would choose. I wanted to know. But I mean, it's just a job. It's just a job.

ROB. It seems like it meant a lot to you.

JAMES. That's one way to put it. Before Nessa was born, my career was *everything* to me. But, I guess I made that pretty obvious. I worked so hard and people liked me and I knew what I was doing. When my wife left…I quit. I loved that job, but Nessa's my kid and my responsibility. And now I'm working some low-level position that I'm overqualified for with good hours but like one third of the pay and my resume is screwed and I'm wearing this stupid shirt and everyone was going to be here tonight and you were helping and I'm being a jerk and…

(Beat.)

And I kinda…needed some help.

ROB. Well, it's starting to look like I kinda needed some advice.

JAMES. Being trapped in a bathroom really makes us a sentimental bunch, huh?

ROB. Yeah the stench of bleach and questionable color scheme really cultivates my emotional side.

> (**JAMES** *has been working on the diaper this whole time and leans back, frustrated.*)

JAMES. This thing will not go on! It's not sticking.

> (**ROB** *leans over and studies it.*)

ROB. Where are the little flappy things? Shouldn't this one have those too?

JAMES. It's on backwards. It's on backwards.

> (*Frustrated, he works on getting the diaper back off and flipping it over.* **ROB** *watches him.*)

ROB. Your daughter's really lucky, James.

> (**JAMES** *smiles, finishes with the diaper, and picks up his baby.*)

JAMES. Your wife's really lucky too. With or without new countertops.

> (**ROB** *gives him a nod and turns to leave, but turns back around. He hands* **JAMES** *Nessa's pants.*)

ROB. Good luck getting those clasps snapped back in.

> (*He turns to exit. Re-snapping the pants had not occurred to* **JAMES**, *and his face falls. He turns, horror written on his face, and –*)

> (*Blackout.*)

LOVE IS BLIND

Aiko Lozar

LOVE IS BLIND was first produced at Carlsbad High School in December 2018 by the student production club, directed by Aiko Lozar.

LOVE IS BLIND won, was workshopped and produced at the Joan Kroc Theater in January–February 2020 by the 2019 California Playwrights Project, directed by Ruff Yeager.

LOVE IS BLIND won, was workshopped and produced digitally for International Thespian Society's NextGen Playworks, dramaturged by Nick Pappas and directed by Stewart Hawk.

LOVE IS BLIND was produced virtually during the 2020 Virtual International Thespian Festival.

CHARACTERS

AMBER
AMBER'S MOM
BLAKE
BLAKE'S MOM
YOUNG BLAKE
YOUNG AMBER
STUDENTS
CANDY
DIANA
GEORGE
TEACHER
CLAY
RAINA
BULLIES
ALEXAVIER

Scene One: Intro

(The stage is black, minimalistic. The cast, facing upstage, beats their chests in a pattern of "bu dum, bu dum," like a human heartbeat, slowly at first, then gaining speed.)

ALL. The year is 2121 –

*(A spotlight appears, illuminating **AMBER**, a mousy, bookish teenage girl who plays by the rules.)*

AMBER. And my name is Amber.

Now, the fact that my mom named me after a color

is kind of ironic

because well,

(Tucking hair behind her ears.) I don't see color anymore.

*(A second spotlight illuminates **AMBER'S MOM**, a middle-aged, tired woman with a bit of magic in her eyes. She sits typing at her desk.)*

My mom swore that –

AMBER'S MOM. I'm sure the color of the sunset is

amber.

AMBER. Before they, you know, decided that it would be better

to implant a little chip in all of our brains

that used an algorithm put in place

by the best two scientists

in the entire world,

to find matches for us boys and girls.

> *(The entire stage lights up now, displaying rows of* **STUDENTS** *smiling. They act like children.)*

Through height and voice and personality,

passion and compatibility.

> *(The* **STUDENTS** *dance or play a game with each other, smiles still plastered on their faces. A couple* **BOYS** *play with* **BOYS** *and* **GIRLS** *with* **GIRLS**.*)*

And well, I mean, I guess their system

has a ton of credibility.

But this chip,

that was in our brains since birth,

that compares all of our worth,

it took away this thing called color.

And you aren't supposed to see "color" until you meet your soulmate,

> *(Everyone pauses.)*

the person who loves you for you because *(Confused.)* that's what the chip says.

And a blast of color into everything without any more wait.

> *(Everyone unfreezes, runs to another partner, and dances with them.)*

It's really fantastic, I mean yes, it's great,

that they eliminated these things called "war" and "divorce."

> *(The **STUDENTS** point finger guns at each other and fall to the ground.)*

But my mom, of course,

> *(The stage dims except for **AMBER** and **AMBER'S MOM**.)*

she said it also got rid of this thing called –

AMBER'S MOM. Falling in love.

AMBER. She's the only one who remembers it.

Now, the way she describes it, it sounds like magic.

She told me it was truly tragic –

AMBER'S MOM. That our new technology

took that opportunity –

AMBER. Away from me.

But the way I see it,

I hate tripping and falling.

> *(Full lights return. The **STUDENTS** stumble and fall –)*

ALL. Ring, ring, ring!

> *(And run offstage. **AMBER'S MOM** exits.)*

AMBER. Why would I want to fall in something called... love?

I don't understand it.

It messes with my brain.

I don't like thinking about it,

it gives me a migraine.
But that was before, before my best friend
Blake Colby –
well –
here's...
here's my story:

Scene Two: Meet Blake

*(**BLAKE**, a quirky jokester who has big dreams, a disregard for school, and a dark past, enters.)*

BLAKE. Hey, Amber, I have a riddle for you.

AMBER. Well. Hello to you, too.

BLAKE. Can I say it?

AMBER. *(After a beat.)* Shoot.

BLAKE. What's black, and white, and red all over?

AMBER. *(Jokingly.)* Red? Isn't that a color or something?

BLAKE. That's one way of looking at things.

AMBER. So, what's the answer?

BLAKE. *(Barely containing his laughter.)* Well, I forget.

*(The stage dims except for **AMBER**. **BLAKE** freezes.)*

AMBER. I remember the day we met.

Blake Colby has been my best friend since second grade.

*(A spotlight illuminates **YOUNG AMBER** and **YOUNG BLAKE**, trading cards and laughing.)*

Oh, the days in the shade,

where we played and played.

The cards we used to trade,

never afraid.

Let me tell you a little bit about Blake.

He was thoughtful without being thoughtful

and careless at the same time of being careful.

(**AMBER** *ruffles his hair.*)

AMBER. He was a mess of contradictions, my best friend.

(Beat.) But nothing was ever complicated with him.

It was always black and white and not gray.

Everything was always okay.

Because he always knew exactly what to say.

But he's uh, what they call...

anti-establishment.

Hated school, called it a punishment.

Did everything to get outta class.

And when he's in, he's the kid that always asks:

YOUNG BLAKE. Can I have a pencil...or a pen?

AMBER. The kid who cracks jokes

every now and then.

He's not a bad boy, no, not really.

More of a "class clown."

But I guess what I like about him

is that I've never seen him frown.

I've known him forever and a half,

I know things about himself he would never tell himself.

(Slowed.) How when his sister, Sydney, died,

he cried and cried and cried.

But no, I've never seen him frown.

I always made fun of him –

the way he shied away from conflict,

never really direct,

always quick to deflect

and protect

his feelings.

Head full of big dreams but would never say them.

Had this fear of people leaving...

>   (**AMBER** *shakes her head, as if making a realization but disregarding it.*)

My best friend Blake Colby,

(*Blunt.*) nothing was ever complicated with him.

>   (*Full lights return.* **BLAKE** *unfreezes and appears next to* **AMBER**, *tapping her left shoulder, but he is to her right.* **AMBER** *has to make a full circle before seeing him.*)

BLAKE. Are you going to class?

AMBER. Do you really have to ask?

BLAKE. Come on, stay outside!

Smell the dew on the grass.

AMBER. I'm gonna be late, Blake,

>   (**AMBER** *heads stage right.*)

I don't have another hall pass.

>   (**STUDENTS** *begin crossing the stage as if heading to class.*)

BLAKE. (*Following her.*) I suppose I'll go too.

AMBER. That's the spirit.

BLAKE. Where to? Where to?

AMBER. I have math class in exactly two minutes.

BLAKE. At least it's no physical fitness.

Do you want some candy?

AMBER. *(Laughing.)* You've got a one-way ticket to obesity.

BLAKE. And you've got a one-way ticket to being late.

Doesn't class start at eight?

> (**STUDENTS** *begin rushing. The atmosphere is "alive"* – **STUDENTS** *eating, pantomiming chatter, etc.*)

AMBER. What about you?

BLAKE. Eh, I'd rather wait.

AMBER. And skip class?

BLAKE. I've got a pass.

AMBER. Forged?

BLAKE. Hah, by George.

> (**GEORGE**, *a cliché trope of a deep-voiced, fist-bump "guy" friend, passes* **BLAKE** *and gives him a high five – up top then down below.*)

(Defensive.) It only cost me a couple of bucks.

AMBER. Excuse me while I get my education.

BLAKE. Excuse me while I make a donation

to the Blake-Colby-needs-a-break foundation.

AMBER. *(Rolling eyes.)* See you later, Blake.

BLAKE. Wait!

Amber,

today, you, uh,

you look great.

*(Beat. It's awkward. Everything freezes except for **AMBER**.)*

AMBER. Ringing in my ears and my face got hot.

What's this feeling that's making my stomach knot?

My head gets dizzy with all the air the world's got.

I think I mumbled out thanks

and I walked away –

*(**AMBER** walks away.)*

I didn't know what else to say.

*(**AMBER** walks close to the audience.)*

He's been my best friend since second grade.

Why did that seem to change?

Maybe it's the way

he said something he never used to say.

He would always tell me,

jokingly:

YOUNG BLAKE. *(Peaks head in stage left.)* You look uh...uh...ugly!

BLAKE. *(Not hearing **AMBER**, walking up next to her.)* And she would reply

with something snarky and sly.

YOUNG AMBER. *(Peaks head in stage right.)* Talk much?

AMBER & BLAKE. And such and such.

(Beat.) It was our thing.

AMBER. But, I guess, so was cards.

BLAKE. And shooting stars.

AMBER. Or playing queen and king.

BLAKE. *(Chuckles.)* Our thing.

(He exits.)

Scene Three: Discover Color

>   (**STUDENTS** *filter in and sit in desks on platforms.* **TEACHER** *enters.*)

AMBER. *(Shakes head.)* I put it in the back of my mind;

I have bigger things to worry about.

I have a big test

that's been making me stressed.

I just have to do my best.

My heart beating,

my heart beating,

I hear my heart beating.

>   (*Everyone beats their chest in a pattern of "bu dum, bu dum," like a human heartbeat.*)
>
>   (**AMBER** *tries to find a seat, but all the ones on the platforms are taken. The only one left for her is center stage on the floor.*)

My head swarming with his eyes.

>   (**AMBER** *catches herself and laughs uncomfortably.*)

No!

I meant

my head swarming with

things I need to study for.

Things like –

STUDENT 1. Equations –

AMBER. Or –

STUDENT 2. Numbers.

AMBER. And through it all, I felt something numb or...

> (**AMBER** *picks up a red pen.* **TEACHER** *passes a test to the* **STUDENTS** *and to the audience.*)

I was suddenly hyperaware

of my pen,

which was

red.

> (*The stage turns completely red. White light resurfaces, but the red undertones remain.*)

Something told me that my pen was red.

I jumped back –

> (**AMBER** *jumps back, looks around.*)

and looked around.

I saw my pen drop on the light gray ground.

Gray – the same color as his eyes.

With Blake –

> (*Everyone looks up.*)

ALL. Everything was black and white and not gray.

> (*Everyone looks back down.*)

AMBER. My heart beating, beating, beating.

> (*Everyone beats their chest in a pattern of "bu dum, bu dum," like a human heartbeat.*)

What is this feeling?

Why is everything else black and white

while my pen is red?

*(**STUDENTS** begin turning in their tests.)*

What's going on inside

my head?

And suddenly,

I felt the area

where my chip was implanted,

I felt it burn

red-hot.

Telling me I'm not; not; NOT

supposed to feel whatever I'm feeling.

That his smile isn't supposed to make me go reeling.

And I know *(Beat.)*

because he's my best friend.

*(**AMBER** is left alone onstage. She finally turns in her test, completely unfinished.)*

Scene Four: Mom's Advice

(The scene enters with **AMBER'S MOM** *typing, stage left, on a desk decorated with pictures of her and Amber. She's tired.)*

AMBER. I think I failed my test, Mom.

AMBER'S MOM. *(Looking up from her computer.)* Okay, okay, calm, calm.

AMBER. I have a question but it's purely theoretical.

Okay, so in a hypothetical:

When you see color, are you supposed to see it one by one?

Or all at once?

AMBER'S MOM. All at once.

AMBER. But what if it's not?

AMBER'S MOM. Then something's glitching in your chip.

Why?

AMBER. *(Beginning to exit, hesitant.)* No reason.

AMBER'S MOM. I don't believe you,

*(***AMBER** *looks back.)*

I, I see it in your eyes.

For everything money can't buy,

I hope for your sake,

you don't misidentify

whatever you think your chip says

with what you actually feel.

Don't let technology mistake you for what's real

*(Looking at **AMBER**.)*

and not real. *(Gesturing to the computer.)*

AMBER. I have to lay down.

I, um, I have a migraine.

*(**AMBER'S MOM** returns to typing, contemplating. **AMBER** walks to her bed.)*

I reach my bed.

The world is red.

I close my eyes

and see his face.

*(**YOUNG AMBER** and **YOUNG BLAKE** cross, dancing and laughing.)*

Open my eyes

and the ceiling –

the ceiling is a hot-star hue

of things we used to do.

The days in the shade,

never afraid.

He's my best friend.

Scene Five: Confrontation

(**BLAKE** *enters.*)

AMBER. Hey, Blake!

(*Catching up with him, they engage in a secret handshake.*)

BLAKE. Hey, Amber.

AMBER. I have a question.

Soooo,

for the sake of theoretical expression –

(**BLAKE** *looks at her.*)

(*Aside.*) He looked at me in succession –

and I couldn't.

I couldn't tell him.

Couldn't explain that I see color when I think of him.

Nothing is ever complicated with him.

(*To him.*) Never mind –

(*Aside.*) I said –

(*To him.*) Have a migraine.

(*Aside.*) He looked at me with concern

(**BLAKE** *looks at her with concern.*)

and the whole world turned.

I thought I saw something,

but it was probably the lights or something.

Anything. It was nothing.

I had a migraine.

ALL. Ring, ring, ring!

AMBER. Yes, it was nothing.

Scene Six: Candy and Andy

(Some **STUDENTS** *filter in, pushing and shoving* **BLAKE** *and* **AMBER**. **DIANA**, *a cliché trope of a girly best friend who loves gossip, meets up with* **AMBER**. **GEORGE** *meets up with* **BLAKE**. *They pull* **AMBER** *and* **BLAKE** *to center stage.)*

DIANA. So, did you hear?

GEORGE. Earth to Blake, check your ears!

DIANA. The whole school just found out.

GEORGE. I don't doubt.

STUDENTS. *(Entering.)* Did you hear?

BOYS. *(Entering.)* Once a year!

GIRLS. *(Entering.)* I'm tear-ing!

DIANA. Do I hear church bells ringing?

GEORGE. Candy and Andy just saw color!

*(***GEORGE** *and* **DIANA** *run to opposite sides of the stage.)*

GEORGE & DIANA. With each other!

(Beat.)

ALL. *(Leaning toward* **BLAKE** *and* **AMBER**.*)* Well?

BLAKE & AMBER. That sounds just…swell.

GEORGE. Here they come!

(Everyone crowds around opposite sides of upstage, **GIRLS** *to stage left,* **BOYS** *to stage right.)*

DIANA. *(Wistfully.)* The lucky two.

That algorithm saved them the trouble before they had to.

Praise science!

> (**AMBER** *walks to downstage right, and* **BLAKE**, **DIANA**, *and* **GEORGE** *walk to downstage left.*)

ALL. Hear, hear!

AMBER. Just what I feared.

> (**CANDY** *walks in upstage left and* **ANDY** *from upstage right, greeting and dancing with each other center stage. They run to meet* **AMBER**.)

CANDY. Oh, Amber, dah-ling!

ANDY. *(To* **CANDY**.*)* You're my dah-ling.

CANDY. I'm blushing.

BLAKE. *(Crossing to* **AMBER**.*)* I'm gagging.

AMBER. *(Aside.)* It was nothing.

CANDY. What a dream!

AMBER. How's it feel? To find your soulmate?

CANDY. The perfect sweepstakes.

You should really, like, try it sometime.

AMBER. *(Bitterly.)* I'll keep that in mind.

> (*The* **STUDENTS** *lose interest. They begin to gossip in little groups.*)

So, are you happy?

CANDY & ANDY. Undeniably.

AMBER. Is that healthy?

CANDY.	ANDY.
Absolutely.	Maybe?

    (**ANDY** *and* **CANDY** *glance at each other awkwardly.*)

AMBER. *(Aside.)* Undeniably happy.

    Sickeningly.

ANDY. Well, see,

    aren't we smiling?

AMBER. That sure is convincing.

TEACHER. Get to class!

    (*Everyone scurries offstage. Some* **BOYS** *stay, listening.* **AMBER** *begins to head offstage, but stops as she hears –*)

BLAKE. *(Sarcastically.)* Better do what she asked.

TEACHER. Did I hear some sass?

BLAKE. No, miss.

    I just wanted to ask

    for a hall pass.

TEACHER. Why's that?

BLAKE. So I won't have to go to your boring excuse for math.

BOYS. Ohhhhh!!

AMBER. *(Laughing uncomfortably, heading to* **BLAKE.**) Blake, always in a hurry.

    We'll scurry.

    He's with me, miss,

    no need to worry.

TEACHER. Amber, honey.

> (**BLAKE** *mouths the words from behind* **TEACHER.**)

AMBER. Yes, miss?

TEACHER. He's a bad influence.

I'll see you in class.

And Amber?

AMBER. Yes?

TEACHER. Don't stress.

You're doing well on your tests,

I must confess,

but I digress.

If you keep hanging around riff-raff –

> (**BLAKE** *laughs.*)

Don't laugh!

Well, I might have to revoke you from the honors program.

BOYS. *(Mockingly.)* The honors program!

> (**BOYS** *and* **TEACHER** *exit.*)

AMBER. She can do that?

BLAKE. God damn.

Less personality than a hologram.

AMBER. Well, I guess I'll see you.

BLAKE. After school?

AMBER. Yeah...cool.

> (*They head off to different sides of the stage, taking one last glance at each other.*)

Scene Seven: Chemistry

*(The **STUDENTS** filter in single file as chairs are brought in factory-style onto the stage. **TEACHER** enters. A light shines on **AMBER**.)*

ALL. Ring, ring, ring!

AMBER. So, we were in class,

listening to the teacher drone on and on about ancient facts.

Something about the old US.

How love caused jealousy; how jealousy caused war.

How lucky we are to not be where they were.

The old presidents

and how they were different from the presents

of the presence

of the present.

The teacher said something about –

TEACHER. Gratitude.

You must have a good attitude.

(Everyone freezes.)

AMBER. Blake rolled his eyes

and looked at me.

*(**BLAKE** rolls his eyes and looks at **AMBER**. It is the only movement onstage.)*

And *(Squealing.)* we made eye contact!

The timing was exact.

I felt my heart contract.

I never saw his eyes in color before.

They were...

ALL. *(Whispering one by one into* **AMBER**'s *ears.)* Blue.

AMBER. They were blue.

> *(The lights tinge blue.* **AMBER** *looks out the window.)*

The color of the sky

that threw

me askew.

And his cheeks –

> *(***AMBER** *turns around, straining to see.)*

His cheeks were red, too.

ALL. Ring, ring, ring!

> *(The* **STUDENTS** *stand up and rush out of class.* **BLAKE** *approaches* **AMBER**.*)*

TEACHER. *(Exiting.)* Don't forget to bring

your presentation things

about 2018.

BLAKE. Amber.

AMBER. Blake.

BLAKE. You okay?

AMBER. The same as yesterday.

BLAKE. Everything is the same as yesterday.

AMBER. Let's go home.

BLAKE. Sounds like an okay way

to end a not-so-okay day.

(They walk to downstage left, near the audience.)

AMBER. Do you really think she'll make me give up the honors program?

BLAKE. Let's not worry about our good ol' satan.

Talk to me.

(They sit. This is their "spot.")

AMBER. *(Aside.)* So, I talked. I talked about the leaves and the trees.

And he talked about his big dreams:

How one day, he's gonna have his very own comedy show.

I told him he's got a long way to go,

and he said:

BLAKE. Well, guess I better start.

AMBER. But I was too busy looking at the invisible stars.

(To him.) Blake, what color are our hearts?

BLAKE. I've heard

they're red.

That's what your mother said.

AMBER. What about when we're...dead?

BLAKE. I suppose they're black and white.

AMBER. *(Aside.)* We looked at each other, then looked away.

(They do so.)

BLAKE. Or maybe it's gray.

AMBER. *(Aside.)* It was nothing.

BLAKE. *(Aside.)* It was the same as yesterday.

(*A long beat.*)

(*Beginning to stand up, to* **AMBER**.) So, I-I've got to go.

AMBER. (*Grabbing his hand.*) I'll see you at your show,

if you ever get around to it.

Hey, one more thing,

before you commit to being a permanent misfit –

something I didn't permit –

what do you think about Andy and Candy?

> (**AMBER** *and* **BLAKE** *look back to* **ANDY** *and* **CANDY**, *arguing.*)

BLAKE. They're happy. Undeniably.

> (**CANDY** *storms off with* **ANDY**, **ANDY** *mouthing to the audience, "Help me."*)

AMBER. Why do you say that?

BLAKE. Well, they're smiling.

> (**BLAKE** *exits.*)

Scene Eight: Smiles (Solo)

(**AMBER** *sits at a desk, upstage center. She's writing.*)

AMBER. Dear Amber – future Amber, that is.

Can we talk for a minute

about smiles?

How they make you feel so

at ease?

How in a blink of a second,

your nightmares can turn into daydreams.

How smiles make you feel nauseous,

and overly stupidly cautious.

Something is telling you in your subconscious

that you can catch more flies.

And I look into your blue, blue eyes

of star-crossed lies,

and all I see is your smile,

sugary sweet liquid syrup

running down your spine,

combining complex veins to look like simple lines.

Smiles are the empty words that aren't spoken when he doesn't call you mine.

(*Nervously.*) What?

I meant:

Smiles are everything in between

the lost time.

They're made of the twisted rose words

of two people on colliding worlds:

A boy and girl.

Smiles are the way you greet someone you don't know.

Tu sonrisa es todo mi tiempo perdido.

Pero, they're also

the way you greet yourself

looking into my mirror in my room.

The way you play make-believe and give your emotions a costume

and some sugar sweet perfume.

Trying to figure out whether or not your reflection has the same smile

of friendship bracelets

and color slits.

Overestimates

of the power of braided thread and doing things just for kicks.

Wondering if it's worthwhile

to keep broken vials

of memories

and a broken promise.

Something about how the world's a stage,

but you're *my* audience.

Blue eyes

strung across my mind,

trying to focus

on things you say are below us.

I'm running on smiles here.

Not sleep, not steam,

but

smiles.

Because smiles are the things you and I have in common.

The things we put in between indents and commas

when you don't know what else to say.

Smiles are the things you do when you realize

the sky is gray,

and not blue,

so I can stare out the window

without thinking of you.

Smiles are the glass sculptures

of friendships

that sure, take your breath away,

but are way too fragile to break.

I'm too tired to sleep.

Can't be kept because they were never mine to keep.

Smiles are everything that reminds me of us and you and them.

Smiles are shattered sewing needles trying to hem

back together a friendship that never ends.

If ignorance is bliss and bliss is utopia, let me live in a plastic world of

smiles

that I'll never know the meaning of.
And they can just be smiles for the sake of smiles,
not for the sake of hate and love.
Let me live in a sugar simple world,
where nothing is colliding
eyes are all gray,
and every single day,
okay means okay.
And I can smile
without it being taken the wrong way.

ALL. *(Offstage.)* Today was the same as yesterday.

Scene Nine: The Anniversary

(**BLAKE** *enters.*)

BLAKE. Amber alert!

Amber alert!

AMBER. Oh hush, you little squirt.

BLAKE. No need to insert

your expert-tease.

AMBER. Blake?

BLAKE. Yes?

AMBER. Shut up, please.

(**DIANA** *and* **GEORGE** *enter.*)

DIANA. Hey, hey, hey, what's the happening? Give me the four-one-one.

GEORGE. Ready to have. Some. *Fun?*

AMBER. What's happening?

(*Beat. They look at her, bewildered, and freeze.*)

The Anniversary! How could I forget?

(*Aside.*) Every year we have a celebration of no threats or regrets.

DIANA, GEORGE & BLAKE. The Anniversary of no war,

no more silhouettes

of being upset.

(**STUDENTS** *and* **AMBER'S MOM** *enter.*)

STUDENT 1. The end of Romeo and Juliet!

(**STUDENT 1** *stands on an upstage platform, holding a red rose.*)

STUDENT 2. The end of killing yourself to be someone else's asset.

(**STUDENT 2** *falls into* **STUDENT 3**'s *arms, who sinks to the ground.*)

STUDENT 3. The end of sinking knee-deep in debt.

AMBER'S MOM. Thus goes the lies the government slings from each day's onset.

STUDENTS. The Anniversary.

The end of love.

AMBER'S MOM. (*Horrified, crossing the stage.*) Oh, the stars above.

(*Everyone [except* **CLAY** *and* **BLAKE'S MOM***] enters and begins to circle* **AMBER.**)

GIRLS. No more –

BOYS. Bang, bang! –

(**BOYS** *shoot the* **GIRLS** *with finger guns, the* **GIRLS** *ducking.*)

GIRLS. War.

BOYS. No more –

GIRLS. Of course –

BOYS. Divorce.

GIRLS. The world at our fingertips.

(*Everyone joins hands.*)

AMBER. (*Bittersweet.*) No more color slits.

BOYS. No more high school flings.

GIRLS. Or school shootings

in 2018.

(Everyone laughs.)

BLAKE. *(Dryly.)* What a dream.

Hey Amber, I got you a present.

AMBER. Not money well spent.

BLAKE. Come on, open it.

(She does.)

AMBER. *(Aghast.)* Are you sure this is meant

for the right event?

BLAKE. It's ironic.

AMBER. It's treason.

BLAKE. It's funny.

*(**AMBER** looks at him.)*

AMBER. And there's a reason.

(Aside.) It was a frame.

It said, "Love Lives."

And it made me relive

all the things I haven't said,

all the secrets I need to give.

It's ironic, he said.

And suddenly the walls were yellow and the ground was green.

The world, the world is so much more beautiful than it seems!

(The lights tinge yellow and green.)

LOVE IS BLIND

It's the color of sunbeams
and dreams –
he's got a lot of those.
I look down at my toes
and try to sense whether or not
he sees the color too.
But all I see in his eyes
is plain blue.

Scene Ten: History

(The **STUDENTS** *enter and gather into a classroom on one side of the stage.)*

TEACHER. Welcome to History One Zero One.

Today, we will talk about the absence of love.

Can anyone guess the first year of the last war?

CANDY. 2070...uh...oh! 2074.

TEACHER. Wonderful, miss, that'll add two points to your class score.

That was the year when everyone's server went dark –

Everyone, write this down, it'll be on the benchmark.

Phones, planes, amusement parks:

all crashed;

social media: trashed;

all hope: slashed.

Boats sank,

and people cried.

Over five billion people worldwide

simply died.

The hospitals were full,

the rations were sold,

the economy plummeted

as people gripped for a stronghold.

BLAKE. *(Mumbling.)* Or that's what we're told.

TEACHER. What happened next?

Can anyone guess?

AMBER. *(Raising her hand.)* Um...people were depressed?

TEACHER. Success! Yes!

People were so obsessed

with these tiny little screens,

that then people felt disconnect-ed

from who they wanted to be.

See, people became lonely.

And people became sad.

People fight because sadness makes them mad.

ALL. People fight because sadness makes them mad.

TEACHER. That's when the United Department of Peace came out with the chip.

It makes people glad.

It was a plan that was ironclad.

Isn't that just rad?

> *(The STUDENTS groan.)*

I get it, I'm trying too hard to have fun and be cool.

Shouldn't do that – after all, this *is* school.

See, the chip meant no more loneliness.

No more war.

Imagine if no one had anything else left to fight for!

We'd be happy.

We'd be content.

We'd stop needing to fill our lives with digital content.

And while we're at it, what if it got rid of affairs?

Of divorce, of break-ups, of cheating, of tears

in perfect pairs?
What if we didn't need to learn how to share
because everyone already had someone who was theirs?
So they knock, knock, knocked
on everybody's door.
What did they say, class?

ALL. Wouldn't you love
the chance to meet the person you were meant for?

*(The lights go dark on the class, and on the opposite side of the stage, the lights go up on **AMBER'S MOM**.)*

AMBER'S MOM. I am determined to not be simply exposition.
I am determined to be an exhibition
of the government's rendition
of a seemingly seamless transition.
See, in a fantastic display of a governmental commission,
my parents designed the device
for the brain's subconscious submission.
This chip
was fully equipped
with the ability to choose your lifelong relationship.
And to ensure government dictatorship?
A little white lie dripped
in the promise of a never-wrong courtship.
It held three secrets:
One: It will find your soulmate.

Two: It will release chemicals to make you in a constant state

of doing whatever the government dictates.

And three: It will control your sight.

See, those who control color control your ability to see the fantastic hues

of twinkling midnights,

of sunlight,

of simple delights

and amber-stricken twilights.

Color is our God-given right.

So, yes, Number Three.

It will control your life.

ALL. The year was 2070

AMBER'S MOM. When *my parents* made this new technology.

They were thirty.

They made it in exchange for government money.

Otherwise, they had nothing.

Geniuses, yet starving.

The leaders of our country struck them a deal:

"Here is five *billion* dollars

in exchange

for the chip,

love authorship,

and yes,

the color wheel.

Now, are you sure the people will comply

when the chip begins to rectify

the chemicals in their mind?"

My parents simply sighed.

> *(Lights up on the classroom as they remain up on* **AMBER'S MOM.***)*

TEACHER. That, children, is why

it is now impossible to cry.

AMBER'S MOM. But the deal had an addendum.

A simple way to lessen

the venom.

My parents' future children will never have to enter the government's version of Heaven.

I will not have to be chipped,

by order of the government.

I would be the singular wire left unstripped,

the singular convict,

the one that slipped.

It was a handshake

and it was a deal.

And for billions of Americans, it was made real.

TEACHER. The year was 2081 when the war was ended,

and the chip was implanted –

yes, the piece of our lives that we take for granted –

they missed no one, no single physician

or musician.

BLAKE. As the class chanted,

   I saw Amber stiffen.

AMBER'S MOM. They tell you, "class,"

   about the '74 Internet crash.

   What a helpful coincidence that by 2081,

   they had a helpful stash

   of chips to

   simply *fix that.*

   The untruths slip

   off of politician lips:

   Here's a chip:

   All it will cost you is your own life's ownership.

   They will tell you, Amber, that –

TEACHER. The implementation was peaceful.

AMBER'S MOM. I was five, and even *I* knew it was evil.

   Amber, it was a slaughterhouse that was somehow legal.

   It amazes me what you have always been taught.

   There really is no beautiful way of saying gunshot.

   After gunshot.

   After gunshot.

   So knock, knock, knock

   on everyone's door.

   "Are you with our new paradise?

   Or are you for war?"

   Amber, I speak for

   the blood that was lost

   that was never accounted for.

TEACHER. And that, class, is why we have our traditions.
When the couples got shuffled
and people became smitten,
why would there need to be war when –

ALL. All was forgiven?

AMBER'S MOM. Thus began the Anniversary.
Amber,
I feel so weary.
I am the only one who remembers.

BLAKE & AMBER. *(Aside.)* And yet people still drink,
go to work and stink
of the beer they throw up in their children's sinks.
They still gamble, and smoke, and choke
on the thoughts they think.

AMBER. The teacher continues.
The class breathes as if nothing is blue.
Dear Blake, out of everyone,
why did I have to have feelings for you?
Sincerely, the girl who just wants to know the truth.

TEACHER. Does anyone know the three rules?

DIANA. *(Raising hand.)* Do not take away anyone's right
to life,
to liberty,
and to the pursuit of soulmates.

TEACHER. Great, great.

GEORGE. The chip must, at all times, be installed in the parietal region of your brain.

TEACHER. Now, what's the last rule that the government mandates?

ALL. If your head hurts, go to the doctor.

TEACHER. Perfect!

Oh, you're all such scholars!

Now, what happens when rules aren't followed?

AMBER. The class said nothing,

and I just swallowed.

I was sure someone would notice that my heart felt hollow.

Outside, I hear the rain from the recent changing of seasons.

I swallow the words from this Garden of Eden.

It tastes like all of the reasons

I don't know what to believe in.

TEACHER. Treason. What happens is treason.

(Beat. Lights down on the classroom as they remain up on AMBER'S MOM.)

AMBER'S MOM. Skip ahead,

my parents mysteriously fall dead.

By natural causes, everyone said.

I can't even imagine their blood's vivid red.

(Long beat.)

I was twenty-seven when I fell in love.

We were a couple of

mourning doves.

His chip glitched,

and mine was never stitched.

No, we could never get hitched,

but I would ditch

any glimmer of this life now

for simply one last kiss.

His name was Resin.

So, try to

give me a reason

why our love was treason.

Give me a reason

why I heard the tick of a –

ALL. Click, click, click –

AMBER'S MOM. And the sing

of a –

ALL. Ring, ring, ring –

AMBER'S MOM. The night they discovered our secret fling.

Goodbye, Resin.

I'll see you in Heaven.

(Beat.)

They decided to *not* kill me.

Oh, you think they cared about their "deal"?

(She scoffs.)

They just wanted to teach me a lesson –

and make *me* forget the whole ordeal.

When I was first chipped,

the first thing I noticed

was that the whole color wheel

was the faint hue of oatmeal.

The red was sepia.

The green was dull.

The colors were never

quite so full.

Guess my parents never could master the colors

that I used to gulp down by the mouthful.

Amber was born in 2105.

A woman, a daughter, a mother, a wife.

And yet the product of gunshots and a colorful life.

I prayed

every day

that she would experience love in the same way –

even if it caused her a lifetime of pain.

ALL. Ring, ring, ring!

Scene Eleven: Blake's Perspective

(Everyone exits except **GEORGE** *and* **BLAKE**.*)*

GEORGE. We interrupt this brief performance

for a brief intermission

on –

*(**GEORGE** exits. Lights return, slightly dimmed.)*

BLAKE. Perspective.

Mine.

My turn to shine.

So, my mom used to tell me this all the time,

ever since I could –

*(Enter **BLAKE'S MOM**, a loud, obnoxious woman who drinks to solve her problems. She dissolves into fits of obnoxious laughter frequently.)*

BLAKE'S MOM. *(To audience.)* Listen up!

Parents,

grandparents,

uncles and aunts.

The very essence

of a child's future inheritance.

Children are dumb.

They laugh and they cry, and frankly,

they don't know better than anyone.

BLAKE. My mom used to say:

BLAKE'S MOM. They can't tell the time of day.

(BLAKE'S MOM moves jarringly, passionate.)

The epitome of teenage angst,

children are stupid!

They are all just kids.

They don't know what's good for them.

BLAKE. My mom said as she took a sip

of something that makes you let go of what-ifs:

(BLAKE'S MOM does so. He mimes what she's doing without an actual flask/bottle.)

BLAKE'S MOM. And they tend to do this thing

where they think

they're the queen and king.

I don't know about you,

but my offspring

won't amount to anything.

BLAKE. She told me this a lot.

BLAKE'S MOM. My little snot –

his name is Blake, by the way –

he always has some little thing

he just has to say.

Drives me insane.

(Beat.)

His sister was better.

BLAKE. I don't doubt her.

BLAKE'S MOM. God, I wish she was here.

BLAKE. *You* told her to disappear!

BLAKE'S MOM. She was an angel,

a precious soul.

BLAKE. *(Getting closer and closer to her.)* You pushed her to

the edge, Mom!

BLAKE'S MOM. A flightless song.

BLAKE. She didn't do anything wrong!

BLAKE'S MOM. Blake has something to live up to.

If he ever has the will to.

BLAKE. Will to what?

I dare you to say!

Don't talk to me about that day.

You don't know the first thing

about living.

You don't know the first thing

about Sydney!

BLAKE'S MOM. Blake, is that you talking?

> *(Everyone hits their chest in a "bu dum" pattern, like a human heartbeat. They stop.)*

BLAKE. *(Suddenly quiet.)* No, Mom.

BLAKE'S MOM. What's wrong?

BLAKE. I was just thinking.

BLAKE'S MOM. Kids, they think they know everything.

Were you eavesdropping?

Go to your room!

> *(**BLAKE'S MOM** exits as **BLAKE** walks slowly to his room.)*

BLAKE. I walk up the stairs and pass my Dress-Up Day costume.

I stand in my bedroom doorway,

I feel a million miles from yesterday.

I laugh.

I like wearing masks.

No one ever asks

anything.

I don't know anything.

You see, I want to cry

but there's nothing.

I hear my dad come home.

> (**CLAY** *enters through the stage-left portal, drunk and tired.*)

He has Mom and me but he's –

ALL. Completely alone.

BLAKE. He pours a glass of something

> (**BLAKE** *mimes pouring a glass, mimicking* **CLAY.**)

to cure the case of what-ifs,

if you catch my drift.

It's okay if you don't.

(Laughing uncomfortably.) No one really does.

My mom already went to bed...

she knows better.

But I was always a go-getter.

I suppose I was just reading the letters

I might one day send to Amber,

if I were to ever tell her about the color.

I hear his footsteps.

    (**CLAY** *begins to step toward* **BLAKE**.)

BOYS. Creak.

GIRLS. Thump.

BOYS. Creak.

GIRLS. Thump.

BLAKE. Freak! Um...

I had lost track of time.

It was twelve o'clock

when I heard the –

ALL. Knock, knock, knock!

BLAKE. My dad never knocks.

I told myself:

Maybe it's Mom,

maybe it's Amber –

maybe,

one day,

things will get better.

I told myself that maybe it's my sister.

She was always a late-night sleeper.

She would help me write my letters.

    (**CLAY** *opens the bedroom door and enters.*)

CLAY. Blake.

BLAKE. Said Clay.

I don't call him Dad anymore

when I'm not to his face.

CLAY. What are you doing still up?

BLAKE. I'm sorry, I'll sleep now.

CLAY. It's twelve o'clock.

ALL. Knock, knock, knock.

CLAY. I said it's TWELVE O'CLOCK!

BLAKE. I'm sorry!

CLAY. There's no room for apologies!

BLAKE. *(Dryly, with a hint of seriousness.)* Forgive me.

CLAY. Don't beg.

It's pathetic.

You're lucky you don't sleep in the attic.

God, why don't you for once just listen?

You just don't have the will to.

BLAKE. I stiffened.

CLAY. Go to bed, son,

or I'll make you.

BLAKE. Will do.

But I *do* have the will to.

CLAY. I said, not to –

> (**CLAY** *brings his arm up to strike but freezes. Everyone beats "bu dum." The lights dim significantly.*)

BLAKE. I don't believe in haunted houses
because ghosts never scared her.
We both got so used to all of our screams
fading into whispers.

    *(**STUDENTS** whisper incoherently.)*

She thought that Dress-Up Day was silly
because she wore a
mask every day.

    *(**STUDENTS** smile.)*

She laughed to fill the cracks of sad
and pushed the pain away.
Ghouls and vampires
never struck me scared.
Because the things I face every day
are monsters when compared.
Her mind was her home,
filled with doors she wanted to leave locked.
Rooms filled with secret tragedies
because no one cared to –

ALL. Knock, knock, knock.

BLAKE. I walked through the doors
of my house all alone.
I never was scared of haunted houses
because she lived in a haunted home.

ALL. She lived in a haunted home.

    (The stage goes black.)

Scene Twelve: Realization

> *(Lights up.* **AMBER** *is sitting on her bed, stage right. She looks through a photo album.)*

AMBER. I was sitting alone in my room,

> looking at the pictures we had of our old Dress-Up Day costumes.

> *(***YOUNG AMBER** *and* **YOUNG BLAKE** *run in,* **YOUNG BLAKE** *dressed as a princess and* **YOUNG AMBER** *dressed as a knight.)*

We dressed

like a princess and a knight,

but you were the princess.

The world was black and white

and not gray.

YOUNG BLAKE & YOUNG AMBER. *(To audience.)* Trick or Treat!

AMBER. But looking back on it, there was so much color

that I missed out on each and every day.

> *(***YOUNG BLAKE** *tackles* **YOUNG AMBER,** *and they fight.* **YOUNG AMBER** *throws orange-and-purple-colored candy toward the audience.)*

And thinking about your new blue eyes,

and the way you close them when you're surprised,

I saw two more colors that I didn't recognize:

Orange

and purple.

> *(***YOUNG AMBER** *and* **YOUNG BLAKE** *freeze. The light tinges orange and purple. Beat.)*

AMBER. Huh. So *that's* the color of those bruises that encircle you, and remind me that you're mortal.

I laugh.

I feel a million miles from yesterday.

(To an unseen Blake.) Blake, I know you're scarred, is that supposed to make me love you less?

(To God.) God, are you joking, is *that* really your best?

(Incredulous.) If that's supposed to make me stop caring about him, I urge you to reassess.

If you think some baggage

is enough to suppress

how I feel about the two-letter word, spelled u-s...

try another guess.

(Aside.) What is this feeling?

I can't explain

what it feels like,

but it feels right.

But wrong.

I can't be in love with him,

I'm not supposed to be.

> *(**AMBER** stands up. **YOUNG BLAKE** and **YOUNG AMBER** run away.)*

I'm a glitch in the system,

a broken algorithm.

Love was written

out of existence.

They told me love caused wars.

They told me that love made people get hurt.
But if love is color and *this is love*,
let me be sore,
and adore and endure
a thousand wars.

    (Beat.)

My mom told me
falling in love
was something taken away from me.
Being in love was something I could never be,
but something everyone needs.
And something is telling me
I've been falling in love for a long time,
but something in my mind
was keeping me from realizing it.

    (The lights tinge white.)

And suddenly, a piercing white headache
makes my head break.
To go to the doctor is the worst decision a Juliet could make.
Love hurts, that's what they told me.
But if love hurts, then *why am I still so happy?*

    (A long beat.)

Did you know?
To love "because" and not "despite"
is the recipe for a red rose

and green meadows.

Did you know that black and gray are still the colors of shadows?

And did you know

that love feels like someone is breaking your heart by making it too

full?

Scene Thirteen: Confession

(**BLAKE** *enters, and* **AMBER** *walks up to him.*)

AMBER. My headache dulls as I listen to my pulse.

I walk up to him in my color-crossed world

and see his white hair and black clothes.

I notice the way his smile is more colorful than a rainbow.

My head hurts in ways he'll never know.

BLAKE. Amber.

AMBER. Through my headache,

I respond:

Blake.

BLAKE. You will never believe in a million years,

through all the smiles and tears

that we've been through –

AMBER. Yeah?

BLAKE. Amber, did you know my eyes are blue?

AMBER. You see it, too?

(*Everyone "bu dum"s, and* **BLAKE** *freezes.*)

My heart stopped beating. Nothing was ever complicated with him.

I *knew* that love can be reciprocated.

I *knew* that war wasn't created

because of the things they stated.

Their views are outdated.

God, I'm fascinated

from how they illustrated

love.

He loves me.

He loves me not.

Where was that from?

Some forget-me-nots?

I forgot.

Love is black and white and red all over.

ALL. His eyes are blue.

AMBER. *(Extremely happy.)* I guess he sees it too.

BLAKE. *(Unfreezing.)* So, there's this new girl. Raina.

    (**AMBER** *says nothing.*)

You might've seen her around.

    (**AMBER** *doesn't move.*)

Well, when I saw her, I looked at the ground

and I looked around,

and I felt the whole world break down.

Everything was color.

I found...

I found my soulmate, Amber.

    (*Beat as* **AMBER** *processes.*)

AMBER. My rejection happened in a

few seconds,

and a million and one things happened.

I stopped fighting my headache, so I could think clear.

White dots seemed to appear.

There goes the hue of your bruises.

> *(Purple disappears.)*

(Frantically.) There goes the green, the orange –

> *(Green disappears, then orange.)*

There goes my grasp on what the truth is.

There goes the yellow of the laugh that is distinctly his.

> *(Yellow disappears.)*

I think I should wave it goodbye,

but then red is gone in the blink of your no-longer-blue eyes

> *(Blue disappears, then red.)*

that were never…

mine.

And suddenly, everything was black

> *(The lighting plunges.)*

and white

> *(The stage slowly returns to simply white-lit.)*

and gray.

The ground was gray,

my skin was gray,

ALL. His eyes were gray.

> *(Everyone but **AMBER** exits.)*

Scene Fourteen: What's Red (Solo)

> *(Is **AMBER** speaking more to the audience or to herself?)*

AMBER. And the sky was gray, and not blue.

So I could look out the window and not think of you.

So I wonder,

what's black

and white

and red all over?

I never liked that riddle.

Because what's red?

Red is the feeling of blood underneath my veins,

red is the feeling of happiness rushing to my brain.

Red is the way I feel when you close your eyes

when you're surprised.

Red is the feeling of cries and lies

and all the hope and dreams money can't buy.

Red is the feeling of the head-spinning, ear-ringing, singing-while-skipping

feeling of love.

Knowing that someone is looking down from above,

telling me that all I'm feeling is a glitch in the system,

to just listen to our

twisted placebos for wisdom,

that love isn't love if it wasn't planned by an algorithm.

But through all the black and white

and not feeling right,

through the lack of color,

black skies and white thunder,

with all the wonder a person could utter:

We can learn about rainbows,

but we'll only see shadows

of lines across grayscale skies.

Ignorance is bliss, but I don't want to live in a lie.

And, I may not see color; not anymore.

But I still live in a colorful world.

Blue is the feeling of knowing that you'll never be mine.

Yellow is how I feel when you make me happy for the first time

in a long time.

Orange is sunset cupids

and purple is the feeling of all of your secret scars and bruises

and technology muting out God-given music,

and beneath all the confusion:

Red.

It's all red.

And I don't really mind.

And even though, even though

you can never be mine,

I still thank you for making me fall in love with you

and not the way your numbers match up with my numbers,

not the way our personalities mesh

according to some equation that can't remember what we remember.

I'm stuck in a world of colorless amber and embers.

Je crois que je suis amoureux de toi,

I stand here as the country's biggest flaw,

and I'm thanking you

for making me fall in love with you

even though it's complicated.

>*(Lights down.* **AMBER** *exits.)*

Scene Fifteen: Blake's Perspective: Raina

(Lights up.)

BOYS. *(Offstage.)* Pause.

GIRLS. *(While in motion.)* Re-re-re-wind.

> *(**STUDENTS** "rewind" as they enter and backpedal onto the opposite wall. The lights flicker. **BLAKE** enters.)*

BLAKE. It's easy, you find,

to hate me blind,

when you don't have any

perspective.

Respectfully and respective-ly,

I was walking down a one-way street,

stuck in some daydreams

about maybes.

BULLY. Outta my way!

> *(**BULLIES** push past **STUDENTS**. They drop their books.)*

STUDENTS 1, 2 & 3. Whatever you say.

BULLIES. Honk, honk!

STUDENTS. 'Scuse me!

BULLIES. Beep, beep.

STUDENTS. Forgive me.

> *(**CLAY** and **BLAKE'S MOM** enter.)*

BLAKE. If this isn't war –

CLAY. *(In* **BLAKE***'s head.)* Don't beg, it's pathetic –

BLAKE. Then what the hell is?

I'm sick of this.

God, I can't wait to make it big.

What wouldn't I give

for one motherly compliment?

BULLIES. Traffic jam! *(One by one.)* Bam, bam, bam!

(The **BULLIES** *push the* **STUDENTS.***)*

BLAKE. I miss when we were children.

I can't wait to be an adult.

I hear the echoes of a failed test

and my mother saying –

BLAKE'S MOM. Parents know best.

BLAKE. I haven't been feeling myself lately

and I wanted to talk to Amber.

I got to my locker.

(He reaches his locker.)

If I could, I would've stopped her.

I heard a –

(Enter **RAINA**, *a ditzy, insane girl, whose voice drips like sugar water.)*

RAINA. SHRIEK! OH, EM, GEE,

WHERE IS HE?

WHO'S THE LUCKY OWNER OF THE NEXT BAJILLION DATES?

BLAKE. I couldn't help feeling bad for whatever idiot will be her soulmate.

RAINA. I SEE COLOR!

BLAKE. I don't know her.

Wait, why is the color I saw with Amber

becoming duller?

RAINA. IT'S YOU.

>   *(Everyone "bu dum"s and faces the audience.)*

>   (**RAINA** *pushes through the crowds,* **GEORGE** *and* **DIANA** *following, to get to* **BLAKE.** *They push him upstage center.)*

GEORGE. Lucky guy!

DIANA. Lucky lady.

RAINA. I'm so glad I get to meet you, finally.

GEORGE. His name's Blake.

BLAKE. There must be a mistake.

RAINA. Why, darling?

>   *(Everyone freezes.)*

BLAKE. I couldn't stop gagging.

I wanted to cry but there was nothing.

I've been seeing color for a while now but I haven't said anything.

Geez, does this migraine sting!

This can't be happening.

>   *(He heads to his* **MOM.***)*

I told my mom

what was wrong,

but all she said was –

BLAKE'S MOM. Sydney was a flightless song.

BLAKE. I would tell my dad,

> *(He heads to CLAY.)*

but I didn't want Amber to worry

about the bruises blooming.

They were purple, but she didn't know that.

Yes, I would tell my *dad*,

but all I have is *Clay*,

and he would just say –

CLAY. You're making war!

BLAKE. I can't do this anymore!

I've always been anti-establishment.

But nothing was ever complicated

until *I* said that stupid compliment!

I needed *(Voice catching.)* –

I needed to protect us from treason.

She'll never understand the reason.

I met the love of my life but –

ALL. She isn't your soulmate.

BLAKE. *(Returning to upstage center.)* So clean slates.

I put on a blank face.

I like wearing masks.

So if anyone asks:

RAINA. I like,

    j'adore you, babe.

BLAKE. I'll say:

    Same.

ALL. The year is 2121.

        (**AMBER** *enters. They make eye contact.*)

BLAKE & AMBER. But so much has changed.

        (*The stage fades to black.*)

Scene Sixteen: O'clock

> (**AMBER** and **BLAKE** sit on their respective beds. Lights up.)

AMBER. So here I am, it's six o'clock,

> (Everyone "click, click, click"s. They do so whenever the time changes – thus, whenever **BLAKE** or **AMBER** say a number.)

and if I could, I would bottle up the feeling of being in love

and sell it for three hours a pop.

BLAKE. I hit my alarm clock

until it stops.

I stretch the sleep from my eyes,

AMBER. And I tell myself that today I won't cry.

BLAKE & AMBER. Today is going to be the same as yesterday.

AMBER. It's seven o'clock.

I'm telling my mom that we're late,

but aren't we always?

> (**AMBER** jumps into a pseudo-car with her **MOM**, moving to where **STUDENTS** are sitting at their desks.)

I'm in the car.

I think I see the invisible stars.

But I'm too busy studying

to look that far.

> (**BLAKE** heads to the desks and sits.)

BLAKE. It's nine.

    And it's one of those times

    when I don't really know

    how it's defined.

    I sneak glances at my friends,

> *(He fist-bumps* **GEORGE.***)*

    wondering when it will end.

    Life is way too short,

    but I'm not thinking about that.

    I don't have the time.

    Eleven eleven.

    Make a wish.

    I have too many to waste on this.

    Yo no quiero un deseo.

    I'm closing my eyes and thinking about saying so.

    But instead, I tell people I made a wish.

    It's incredible how many times I lie in a day.

    Today is the same as yesterday.

AMBER. It's one p.m.

    Vamos a la clase de español.

    She takes roll

    and I pretend

    to be present.

    It's amazing how many times I pretend in a day.

    Tomorrow will be the same as today.

    Or I'm in biology,

where *nobody* knows what they're doing.

Everyone looks to me.

>   *(They do so briefly.)*

I am just as confused as they are,

because I'm too busy looking at the invisible stars.

But I don't show it.

I like wearing masks;

I like to pretend.

ALL. Ring, ring, ring!

BLAKE & AMBER. Two thirty.

Finally.

Definitely.

BLAKE. On good days,

I walk to our spot

>   *(**BLAKE** and **AMBER** walk to their "spot." Everyone exits but them.)*

and I talk

to my best friend

about our days.

We look at the sky,

and the wind in our face

makes us believe that things might be okay.

Sometimes we don't say anything,

and we just bathe

in knowing we're going to be okay.

This is mi deseo.

AMBER. He throws his head back

when he laughs.

> (**BLAKE** *does so.*)

Those are the best days.

> (*They go back to their bedrooms.*)

I promised myself I wouldn't cry today,

but it's the same as yesterday.

I want to feel like myself again

It's twelve a.m.

Breathe in.

I know what my wish is.

BLAKE. Before I know it, it's six o'clock.

And if I could, I would bottle up the feeling of being in love and sell it for three hours a pop.

Because there's not enough time in the day.

ALL. Today will be different than yesterday.

BLAKE. We all tend to say.

My alarm clock

tells me I'm late.

AMBER. Until one day, everything was different.

AMBER & BLAKE. But (s)he will never know it.

Scene Seventeen: Finale

(**AMBER** *and* **BLAKE** *remain in their beds, but time has passed.*)

ALL. The year is 2125.

(**AMBER** *has changed. Her glasses are gone. She is more giggly, more flighty. She doesn't like to think too hard about things. Has she forgotten all about love?*)

AMBER. My mom says I used to have migraines, but I don't remember them.

Something about love or something I don't quite get.

(Gesturing to him.) Oh, there's Blake!

Blake and I have been best friends since forever.

He's basically like my brother.

I couldn't ever think of him any other way.

My mom said, one day, when he found his soulmate,

(**RAINA** *enters.*)

I changed.

(Giggling.) But I have no clue what she's talking about.

(Pause, then a sudden burst of energy.) I can't wait to see color!

My mom says it's a hoot.

I wonder which color is Diana's new boots.

Life is so simple.

Nothing is ever complicated.

BLAKE. Today is the same as yesterday.

AMBER. Sometimes we look at each other for a second too long.

> *(They do so, but* **RAINA** *pulls* **BLAKE** *back to look at her.)*

And I think I see something,

but it's probably just the lights or something.

(Hopeful.) Anything.

(Shaking it off.) It was nothing.

I don't want a migraine.

One day, I was sitting in my bed

and I heard a –

> *(***ALEXAVIER**, *the pretty-boring-but-not-that-bad delivery man, enters and knocks on her door.)*

ALL. Knock, knock, knock.

AMBER. Hello?

ALEXAVIER. Hello, I have a package for –

AMBER & ALEXAVIER. Everything was color.

I found my soulmate.

AMBER. A rush of color into everything

without any more wait.

It's fantastic, I mean, truly, it's great!

BLAKE. We met up one day.

> *(***BLAKE** *and* **AMBER** *meet up center stage.)*

Ever since I met Raina, the world has been more gray,

> *(***RAINA** *nods enthusiastically to the audience.)*

BLAKE. More dull,

my heart never full.

Sure, I see color, but nothing like with Amber.

I think I'm the only one who remembers.

I knew she got into the college of her choice after being in the honors program

> *(The **TEACHER** walks in and hands **AMBER** a certificate.)*

and I got a big comedy show with George, my main man.

> *(**GEORGE** walks in and gives him a "bro hug.")*

Successful and smiling,

but I don't think we were happy.

> *(From stage right to left: **ALEXAVIER**, **AMBER**, a gap, **BLAKE**, **RAINA**. They are lined up straight, facing the audience.)*

RAINA. His arm was around me,

ALEXAVIER. And my arm around her.

AMBER. I forget what I once imagined we were.

> *(**BLAKE** and **AMBER** turn to face each other.)*

BLAKE. Hey, Amber.

AMBER. Hey, Blake.

BLAKE. I see you found your soulmate.

AMBER. I did.

BLAKE. Are you happy?

AMBER. Undeniably.

> *(Everyone "bu dum"s.)*

(Aside.) His eyes were blue.

The same color of the sky

that threw me askew.

A hot-star hue.

I thought I remembered a dream or two

about me falling in love with you.

But I forgot

because I got...

a migraine.

> (**AMBER** *makes her way to the upstage platform. As* **AMBER** *is walking, she makes eye contact with* **BLAKE**, *but he gestures to* **ALEXAVIER**, *who has been trying to get* **AMBER***'s attention.*)

> (**AMBER** *turns to* **ALEXAVIER**, *and* **ALEXAVIER** *hands her a rose. Everything dims except for a spotlight on her.*)

Amber is the feeling of big tests

and hall passes

and skipping classes.

Amber is the way I feel when I think of you.

And my name is Amber.

Now, the fact that my mom named me after a color

is kind of ironic because well,

I don't see color.

Anymore.

> *(Fade to black.)*

SUNDAY AFTERNOON GIN

Josie Palmarini

SUNDAY AFTERNOON GIN was produced virtually during the 2020 Virtual International Thespian Festival.

CHARACTERS

MRS. WACKETT – (36) A cheerful chatterbox of a woman who spends her time gossiping and spreading rumors about fellow women in the neighborhood.

MRS. SEABROOKE – (34) Quieter than all of her friends. She is insecure and often goes along with whatever her friends say.

MRS. POPLAWSKI – (37) A rather judgmental and mean woman who thinks that a woman's place is in the kitchen and the home only.

MRS. QUIGLEY – (38) A fiery and willful woman who often judges other people for their moral ideals and feels that she is the height of morality.

SETTING

Suburbia; back porch

TIME

1960s; Summer or Spring

(MRS. POPLAWSKI, MRS. QUIGLEY, MRS. SEABROOKE, and MRS. WACKETT sit outside playing gin and drinking ice tea under a porch umbrella. There is a tenseness in the air. All of the WOMEN seem to be holding back. Their movements are slow, calculated, and almost fearful. This is the same with their words. WACKETT turns to QUIGLEY with the plastic container of ice tea.)

WACKETT. Mrs. Seabrooke, darling, would you care for another glass of Mrs. Quigley's delightful ice tea?

SEABROOKE. No thank you, Mrs. Wackett. *(Whispers.)* Honestly, I feel as if it might be giving me a bit of a belly ache.

QUIGLEY. Well, that's odd, because I've had nothing, but *my* ice tea all day and *I* feel perfectly fine. Perhaps, Mrs. Poplawski's stuffed celery is to blame. It did look rather old.

POPLAWSKI. That's impossible. I purchased that celery just yesterday. It's fresher than a newborn baby. Might I suggest, Mrs. Seabrooke, that your very own tea cakes may be the culprit? I told you they were a bit on the sweet side.

SEABROOKE. *(Defensive.)* Oh, I don't think –

WACKETT. *(Cuts her off. Excitedly.)* Aren't I just pleased as punch that we were all able to get together this week? I've missed you girls!

POPLAWSKI. Absolutely! *(Whispers.)* I love my children, but I've been practically starved for some *adult* conversation.

*(The **WOMEN** laugh.)*

WACKETT. Well, in that case, you'll never guess what I heard at last week's Ladies Group!

QUIGLEY. Is it about that new family down the block? The Reynolds?

SEABROOKE. Or is it about little Cynthia Johnson? Have they finally found out who the father is?

POPLAWSKI. Oh, I know! Is it Bobby Rogers? *(Whispers.)* I heard rumors that he was a *(Whispers.)* – *homosexual*.

WACKETT. No, no, and no. It's about Sarah Williams. Do you all know who that is?

POPLAWSKI. *(Picks up another card.)* Yes yes. We *all* know Sarah.

WACKETT. *(Leans in.)* I heard that little Miss Williams is having herself an *affair*.

QUIGLEY. Affair? But, she's not married! Why! She doesn't even have a boyfriend!

WACKETT. Apparently she's the mistress of a *married* man.

SEABROOKE. Who?

POPLAWSKI. She already told you! Sarah Williams!

SEABROOKE. No! I meant who's the man?

WACKETT. That's the part I don't know. All I know is that he lives here. In the neighborhood.

QUIGLEY. Well, whoever he is, his *wife* should be ashamed of herself. Any woman who can't keep her husband happy, well, all I'll say is, she deserves whatever happens.

*(All of the other **WOMEN** nod in agreement. They play in silence for several seconds after. The tenseness in the air has become heightened. All of the **WOMEN** are thinking*

the same thing. **SEABROOKE** *takes a peak at* **QUIGLEY***'s cards, as* **QUIGLEY** *takes a sip of ice tea. After drinking the tea she makes a face, like the tea is bad, but smiles anyway and takes another sip.* **POPLAWSKI** *begins to bite her nails, but quickly stops when she realizes that* **WACKETT** *is watching her.* **WACKETT** *smiles tightly.)*

WACKETT. Mrs. Poplawski, I forgot to ask, how's Jonathan?

POPLAWSKI. *(Picks up the card and examines it before placing it back down in the pile face up.)* Jonathan's well. He and I played Scrabble last night. He beat me with the word "zoo"! Honestly, I don't know how he does it! Coming up with all those words!

SEABROOKE. Scrabble is such fun! We *just* have to play some time!

QUIGLEY. *(Doesn't look up from her cards as she shuffles. Sarcastically.)* Do we now?

WACKETT. I'm only asking because last time we spoke you said he was spending a lot of late nights at the office and –

POPLAWSKI. *(Cuts her off.)* Yes, well, it's been better lately.

WACKETT. Oh. Good. I'm glad.

SEABROOKE. Good.

QUIGLEY. Good.

POPLAWSKI. Good.

(Silence falls over the **WOMEN.** **POPLAWSKI** *picks up and begins to nibble on a stuffed celery.* **SEABROOKE** *also picks up a celery and begins to put the whole thing in her mouth, before seeing the way* **POPLAWSKI** *is eating it and begins to take little bites instead.* **WACKETT** *holds her cup of ice tea up to her*

face and swishes the liquid around before taking a sip. **QUIGLEY** *attempts a peak at* **POPLAWSKI**'s *cards before speaking.*)

QUIGLEY. Mrs. Wackett, would it be correct of me to say that Michael is out of town on business at the moment?

WACKETT. *(Places her glass back on the table.)* It would.

QUIGLEY. Where exactly did he travel to this time?

WACKETT. Um – *(Tries to think.)* You know I'm not sure. *(Shuffles cards.)* Michael doesn't like to bother me with *silly* little details like that.

SEABROOKE. Didn't he go on a trip last month?

WACKETT. Yes.

POPLAWSKI. That's a lot of trips *(Beat.)* – for an accountant.

QUIGLEY. I wonder why the company would send him on so many?

WACKETT. *(Shuffles the cards in her hands.)* I would imagine it's because they trust him.

QUIGLEY. Yes... *(Beat.)* I suppose so.

POPLAWSKI. I suppose so.

SEABROOKE. I suppose so.

WACKETT. I suppose so.

(*Silence falls over the* **WOMEN**. **SEABROOKE** *begins to swing her legs underneath the table nervously.* **POPLAWSKI** *starts to twirl her hair as she contemplates her cards.* **QUIGLEY** *takes too long to decide whether or not to take the card she picks or put it back down, which visibly irritates* **WACKETT**, *who turns to* **SEABROOKE** *with a fake smile.*)

Mrs. Seabrooke, is Peter still in that bowling league of his?

SEABROOKE. Every Thursday night at seven! You know it's said that his team is undefeated!

POPLAWSKI. I heard that the league was disbanded last month. Not enough men wanted to participate.

WACKETT. That's silly! Then how can Peter be going every Thursday night?

POPLAWSKI. All I know is what I heard.

SEABROOKE. You must have heard wrong then.

POPLAWSKI. I guess I must have.

WACKETT. I guess.

QUIGLEY. I guess.

SEABROOKE. I guess.

> *(Silence falls over the **WOMEN**. **WACKETT** begins to shift in her chair. Crossing her legs back and forth, over and over again. **QUIGLEY** picks up a piece of celery and begins to pick off the raisins. **POPLAWSKI** shuffles her cards back and forth in her hands, trying to determine what order she wants to put them in. **SEABROOKE** taps the table while she thinks, then she turns to **QUIGLEY**.)*

So, Mrs. Quigley, how's Henry's grocery store? I saw a sign in the window that said he got a new kind of fruit: dragon fruit! I've been meaning to come in and try it, but I've been a little nervous.

QUIGLEY. *(Excited.)* Business is booming! And as for the dragon fruit, I will admit that I've been afraid to try it myself. All those spikes! *(Laughs.)*

POPLAWSKI. You know, I don't know anyone in the neighborhood who doesn't shop there. He has the best peaches.

WACKETT. And the strawberries are to die for!

SEABROOKE. Doesn't Sarah Williams shop there?

QUIGLEY. *(Picks a card up.)* I'm not sure.

WACKETT. I'm positive I've seen her there. Ah! I remember! She was buying apples.

QUIGLEY. *(Mutter.)* Really? I hadn't noticed.

SEABROOKE. Yes, well, we all miss things sometimes. Don't we?

WACKETT. Yes.

POPLAWSKI. Yes.

QUIGLEY. Yes.

>*(Silence falls over the **WOMEN**. **QUIGLEY** sniffles, as if to sneeze, but doesn't. **POPLAWSKI** combs her finger through her hair nonchalantly in order to sneak a peek at **WACKETT**'s cards. **WACKETT** sighs and gulps down the rest of the ice tea, and makes a sour face after she does. **SEABROOKE** smiles as she picks up a final card.)*

SEABROOKE. Gin! *(Places cards on the table.)*

POPLAWSKI. *(Throws down her cards.)* Mrs. Seabrooke, you've bested us again! Come on, let's see what your winning hand was this time.

SEABROOKE. A king of hearts, a queen of hearts, a jack of hearts –

QUIGLEY. Oh dear! Mrs. Seabrooke, that's not a jack of hearts! It's a queen of diamonds. *(**SEABROOKE** pulls the cards closer to her eyes.)* I told you to wear your reading glasses.

POPLAWSKI. So, it's not gin.

QUIGLEY. We keep playing.

SEABROOKE. *(Laughs uneasily.)* My my. It does feel as if we've already been at it for hours, doesn't it?

WACKETT. Well, clearly, a king cannot have two queens.

POPLAWSKI. Clearly.

QUIGLEY. Clearly.

SEABROOKE. Clearly.

> *(These words hang in the air. All of the **WOMEN** stare at each other, their bodies tensing. Slowly, they all pick up their cards and resume play, silently this time. Any remote looseness that existed prior is gone. Their movements are stiff and robotic. The **WOMEN** play for several seconds before the lights go to black.)*

THE FIREFLY HOUR

Taylor Lockhart

THE FIREFLY HOUR was produced virtually during the 2020 Virtual International Thespian Festival.

CHARACTERS

MARTIN
BRADY
CLAIRE
MADDIE

(The sun has just nearly set, and the air is sweet and mild. It's a beautiful summer night. Four **TEENAGERS** *dry off on a dock after a full day of swimming in the lake.)*

MARTIN. Brady, I don't know how you didn't swallow the whole lake. You had your mouth open the entire time.

BRADY. Hey, I'm just not very good at swimming.

CLAIRE. You're gonna get sick that way, you know there's bacteria in the water.

BRADY. Don't worry about me, I have a strong immune system.

MADDIE. – And Brady North was found dead in his bed two days later. Doctors just cannot identify what could've caused it.

MARTIN. Hey, have you guys seen my glasses? I swear I put them around here somewhere.

CLAIRE. They didn't fall in the lake, did they?

BRADY. I saw you set them down right –

*(**BRADY** looks around and sees **MADDIE** is wearing **MARTIN**'s glasses.)*

Maddie, give those back to him.

MADDIE. I don't know how you see through these things.

MARTIN. Much better than I do without them.

*(**MARTIN** takes his glasses from **MADDIE**'s face.)*

MADDIE. Well, they're all cloudy. You should clean 'em.

MARTIN. – And Maddie Everest was found drowned at the bottom of a lake tied to a very large and heavy weight.

> (**MADDIE** *sticks her tongue out at him as they all finish drying off.* **BRADY** *stands up and starts grabbing his things.*)

BRADY. Alright, I think Claire and I are going to hit the road. I need to get her home by 11:45.

MADDIE. *(Mockingly.)* Oh, does little Claire still have a curfew?

CLAIRE. *(Mockingly.)* Oh, does little Maddie still have to wear glasses?

MADDIE. You know that contacts hurt my eyes

CLAIRE. Well, you know that my mom's a bitch.

BRADY. – And I can vouch that her mom's a bitch and I don't want to deal with that tonight, so let's get going.

MADDIE. Alright, I'll see you guys later! Drive safe.

MARTIN. Who sets a curfew at 11:45?

CLAIRE. See you, Maddie!

MADDIE. Bye guys!

> (**BRADY** *and* **CLAIRE** *exit offstage, leaving* **MADDIE** *and* **MARTIN** *alone.*)

MARTIN. Wouldn't you think it'd make more sense to make it an even hour like twelve?

MADDIE. Martin, what are you talking about?

MARTIN. Nothing, I'm just mumbling. You know you can leave too if you want.

MADDIE. My car's in the shop so my mom's picking me up tonight.

MARTIN. Well, you could call her.

MADDIE. Are you trying to get rid of me?

MARTIN. No! I mean...kind of. Maybe just a little bit.

MADDIE. What! Why?

MARTIN. You guys just stayed a little longer than I thought you would. I'm used to coming out here on my own. It's kinda my routine.

MADDIE. You come out here and sit on this dock on your own?

MARTIN. Yeah, every night! What else would I be doing?

MADDIE. Watching Netflix or something like a normal person.

MARTIN. Well, you know *Black Mirror* isn't a good stress reliever.

MADDIE. Then watch *The Office*.

MARTIN. Just look over there, I'll show you what I mean.

MADDIE. I see water.

MARTIN. But look at the way the water ripples, and shakes with the earth. It's perfectly illuminated by the moon. It's all just so serene.

MADDIE. I never took you to be so poetic.

MARTIN. If appreciating nature makes me "poetic" then you can call me Shakespeare. Just, take a second to listen. Do you hear that?

MADDIE. Yeah? What is that?

MARTIN. You hear them all the time when you live near the water. Those are bullfrogs, they're over there in that swampy part. Their sound mixes with a sort of ambiance. It's a music you hear best when there's no music playing. It's not a sound or a sight. It's a feeling. If you sit out here, you feel the world around you and it's just...incredible.

MADDIE. It's peaceful.

MARTIN. That most of all. When I'm out here there's no stress that can get to me.

>   (**MADDIE** *thinks for a moment, taking in the world around her before her thoughts drift somewhere else.*)

MADDIE. What stresses you out?

MARTIN. Why would I bring up stress when I'm trying to get rid of it?

MADDIE. Because talking about it is the best way to really get rid of it.

MARTIN. That is absolutely not true. Look, this is a quiet zone, Maddie. If you speak you'll disturb it. Just enjoy the "firefly hour."

MADDIE. The firefly hour?

MARTIN. You'll see.

>   (*As soon as he says that, hundreds of fireflies appear onstage, flying in from stage right, and twinkle like stars.* **MADDIE** *is amazed. She's seen fireflies before, but never in this abundance.*)

They love how murky it is, the lake draws them here.

MADDIE. They're amazing.

MARTIN. They are a sight alright.

>   (*A few seconds go by as* **MADDIE** *stares in awe, but* **MARTIN** *can't help but think about what* **MADDIE** *brought up. Being here with her, he can't help but think about it. He looks at her and then back to the water.*)

Life.

MADDIE. What?

MARTIN. Life stresses me out.

MADDIE. What about life?

MARTIN. I don't know, just life.

MADDIE. *(Sarcastically.)* Well, if we're being that vague life can stress me out too.

MARTIN. *(Sarcastically back.)* You wanna talk about it?

MADDIE. You said talking would disturb the peace.

MARTIN. I did, didn't I? I guess I'm a hypocrite. Let's both just shut up and –

BRADY. *(Offstage, cutting him off.)* Hey did I leave my phone back there?!

> *(CLAIRE enters, followed by BRADY.)*

CLAIRE. Have you guys seen Brady's phone? We can't find it.

> *(MADDIE looks over and sees a phone.)*

MADDIE. Oh, is this it?

BRADY. Yeah, thanks. Hey Martin, do you need anything? You know I always keep spares in my wallet.

MADDIE. Brady, I swear I'm not kidding about the whole found dead thing.

> *(BRADY laughs and they leave. As they exit, a few fireflies disappear. MARTIN watches BRADY and CLAIRE as they leave.)*

I thought you said this was the firefly "hour." Why are they all leaving?

> *(MARTIN doesn't seem to hear her. He's still staring in the direction of where BRADY and CLAIRE left. Something is very clearly bugging him, and MADDIE notices.)*

Are you okay?

MARTIN. How long do you think they'll be together?

MADDIE. Who, Brady and Claire?

MARTIN. Yeah.

MADDIE. I mean, who knows? I guess until something happens.

MARTIN. – And then what?

MADDIE. What do you mean?

(More fireflies begin to disappear.)

MARTIN. What happens after they split.

MADDIE. Well, they might talk or they might not. It depends really.

(Even more fireflies begin to disappear.)

MARTIN. That's what stresses me out.

MADDIE. What? Why are you so concerned about their love life?

MARTIN. I'm not, I mean I want the best for them but their relationship is more like a metaphor to me.

MADDIE. A metaphor?

MARTIN. What happens when we split, does it just depend if we continue to talk or not?

*(**MADDIE** understands what this is about now, and only a handful of fireflies remain.)*

MADDIE. Oh. Is this about me?

MARTIN. I mean, yeah, but not just you. Brady and Claire are leaving as well. I'm a junior surrounded by seniors and I'm a little afraid of what next year's gonna look like without all you guys. I feel like summer is just a calm before the storm. I feel like you're going to forget me.

MADDIE. We can still talk. I'll call you and we can catch up from time to time.

MARTIN. Catch up, yeah. Like, I see my mom talking in the supermarket with a friend she hadn't seen in thirty years. Just a quick, "Wow it's been forever," and then it's back to whatever we were doing before. It's back to our new lives and we leave the old stuff behind. I don't think it's wrong for me to feel like we'll just stop, do you?

    (**MADDIE** *tries to change the subject.*)

MADDIE. You know in my apartment we don't ever see fireflies, but we do see some fireworks from time to time. Only problem is determining when it's a firework or a gunshot.

    (**MARTIN** *laughs in shock for a second before quickly reprimanding her. The fireflies start to reappear around them.*)

MARTIN. You shouldn't make fun of something serious like that.

MADDIE. Yeah, But look at that, you're smiling now. My stupid joke worked.

MARTIN. Yeah but your stupid joke also ruined the mood.

MADDIE. Seems to me like your teen angst ruined the mood.

    (*A slight chuckle, and then they both sit in silence for a very brief moment.*)

Hey, Martin.

MARTIN. Yeah?

MADDIE. You know I won't forget you, right?

MARTIN. Did any of your friends forget you?

(**MADDIE** *freezes, and a few fireflies disappear.*)

MADDIE. I'm not sure.

MARTIN. I'm sorry that was rude to ask.

MADDIE. I mean I haven't kept up with all of them.

MARTIN. What about Sarah? You and her were real close.

MADDIE. We haven't talked much since she graduated.

MARTIN. So my point is valid.

MADDIE. Maybe moving on isn't that bad though?

MARTIN. How?

MADDIE. I think it's natural to meet new people and leave behind some of the older ones.

(**MARTIN** *is stung by this, and more fireflies disappear.*)

MARTIN. I just don't see how that could be –

MADDIE. Maybe the only time we have to see each other is four years, that's still a lot of time and it makes time like this even more valuable. Sarah was my best friend and now you are and after you –

(**MADDIE** *realizes how what she said sounds, and* **MARTIN** *is extremely hurt by her statement but realizes in a way that she's right. Fireflies continue to disappear until only two remain.*)

That came out wrong. What I meant to say was –

MARTIN. I think you should go wait for your mom until she gets here, I'd rather spend the rest of the time back here alone.

(**MADDIE** *is hesitant but can't think of anything to say. She walks away. One of the fireflies flies away with her. Leaving only* *one.* **MARTIN** *walks back and sits on the dock, staring out into the lake and into the audience. He picks up a rock from the bank and skips it.)*

Maybe moving on isn't bad.

(He grabs another rock and skips it.)

Maybe we should all just forget each other and find new people to forget about.

(He chucks another rock, but this time with more force and with more anger.)

Maybe none of this even matters. Maybe we should all just move on straight to death, get the whole thing done and over with!

(He chucks a rock into the water, full force like he's throwing a baseball. There is a large splash. He grabs himself to try and calm down.)

No! I can't live with that. I'm just supposed to say goodbye to a good half of my friends, and then a year later the other half. I'll get a job with new coworkers who will replace everyone else, and then another job, and people will come and go and maybe I'll see my original friends from time to time at some reunion twenty years later where we'll say, "Wow I didn't know you became an electrician." "Hey remember when we were kids and," and, "See you in another ten years," but that's all it is. All it ever will be, all we ever do, we just catch up! I just – I can't live with that! Am I wrong for not being able to live with that? Am I the only person who cares about their friends!

*(**MARTIN**, finished with his angry screaming, looks down, ashamed at his fit and unable to answer his complaints. **MADDIE** is watching from a distance, making sure not to be seen.)*

MARTIN. But then, she's right. That's just how it is. That's how it's always been and how it always will be.

> (**MARTIN** *looks down at the ground in defeat as the last firefly flies away.* **MADDIE** *has a sudden realization as she watches it fly off like the others did.*)

I wonder what it's like for fireflies.

MADDIE. I'd imagine they don't see much of a difference.

MARTIN. I thought I told you to leave me alone.

MADDIE. How could I leave you alone when you just made a good point?

MARTIN. About how everything disappears and you just have to deal with it? Yeah, great point.

MADDIE. No, about those fireflies. They come out here every day and buzz around with their friends but then tomorrow there could be completely different fireflies than the ones they flew with today.

MARTIN. Yeah, so?

MADDIE. So do you ever notice that there are different fireflies?

MARTIN. No, that's impossible.

> (*She walks up and sits down next to him.*)

MADDIE. So, think of people like fireflies. We're all different and our butts don't light up but there's a million of us out there. Sure, you might stop talking with one person but just as soon you'll meet someone new. It's scary leaving people behind, believe me, I know and it scares me that I might forget about you in a few years like my friends forgot about me…but then there's always gonna be a new opportunity with new fireflies, even if they're not the same ones as before.

MARTIN. When did you get so poetic?

MADDIE. What can I say, nature is poetic.

> *(They casually lean up next to each other, staring out into the lake. We suddenly hear a car honk loudly. It breaks the moment, but neither of them wants to leave.)*

That's my mom, I gotta go.

MARTIN. Will you call me, from time to time?

MADDIE. Yeah, I promise.

MARTIN. Then I'll see you around, Maddie.

MADDIE. See ya, Martin.

> *(They hug. They know that life may never bring them together again.)*

Don't stay out here too long, okay?

MARTIN. I'll be fine. I might just sleep out here. Right here under the stars.

MADDIE. But it's cloudy outside?

MARTIN. Then I'll see them in my dreams.

> *(**MADDIE** stares, taking in the moment before walking offstage. As she does, a single firefly comes back onstage and lands next to **MARTIN**.)*

Well hey there bud, what are you doing here. Didn't all of your friends go to sleep?

> *(The firefly flies up and buzzes around **MARTIN**.)*

You're likely to get eaten by a frog out here all alone... but, you don't have to worry about that. I'll stay out here and protect you until you find your friends.

(The firefly continues to buzz around before landing on **MARTIN**'s *finger.* **MARTIN** *watches it for a while before his tiredness gets the best of him. He leans back and lies down, almost instantly falling asleep. The firefly sits on his finger for a few seconds before a few other fireflies appear from stage left, twinkling like stars, and it flies off to join them.)*

(Blackout.)

www.ingramcontent.com/pod-product-compliance
Lightning Source LLC
Chambersburg PA
CBHW072011290426
44109CB00018B/2208